DEWDROPS

DIKSHYA DEBADARSINI

ISBN 979-888555517-3

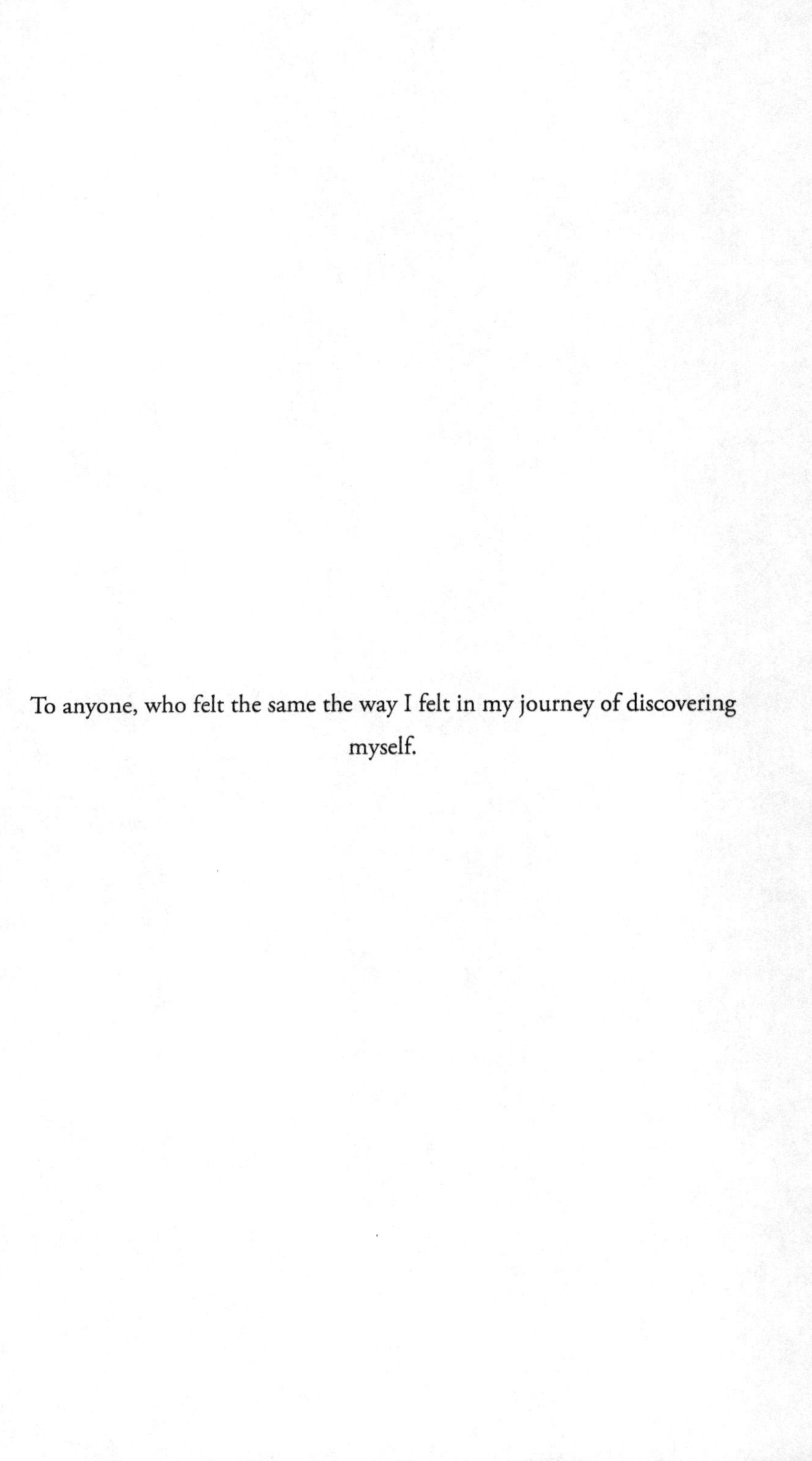

To anyone, who felt the same the way I felt in my journey of discovering myself.

Contents

Contents

Foreword

Dreams locked in my head,
Desires buried inside my chest,
Emotions I felt were silent
Words were scattered
Until I arranged them on sheet,
Wrote and rewrote them with ink
which was frozen in time.
My poems are those words
which I wasn't able to define.

Preface

This book is a collection of poems which I felt during of discovering my life, love and passion.

Her soul was full of light

There was a glow in her eyes

Her smile was enough to spread happiness

Due to all those rejection and lies

darkness had grabbed her

and dragged her into loneliness.

Still, there was a spark of hope

Inside her it was still alive

Nobody could ever take that away

It was enough for her to rise again in her life

Acknowledgements

Thankful to god for all the blessings and for all the circumstances he created in my life which lead me to know my passion and gave me immense strength & creartivity to overcome everything and complete this book

Begin

Beginning starts when you embrace the truth, embrace your soul

Water it everyday with care and wisdom, that's all.

Discover your strength and flaws

Find your faith

Experience true love

Never let your life to get stuck in a pause

Always remember, you are beautiful and unique.

There are so many mystreries in the world

that you have to seek.

Never stop taking chances

Always try to learn and grow

Make new turns, don't go with the flow

Whenever you fall, have courage , be wild

Never let anyone drag you down because it's your life

Horizon

Your thoughts come to me like little drops of rain

Flutters my heart, kisses away all my pain

Your embrace makes me feel warm and secure

Just like the rays of sunlight in the winter

Whenever I am with you, I feel like a different person

Away from this chaotic worls, breaking all the bonds

Far away from the horizon

Transparent

My skin becomes transparent when I am with you

You always manage to see

all the emotions I have curled up inside me

You always caught all my lies

That I try to pass on as true

I don't know what do you feel for me,

Is it your love or just affection

But, I am very sure

Little by little, everyday

you are turning into my addiction.

Solace

She was waiting for that stranger,

sealing all the pain and love inside her

Everyday, she look in the mirror

see herself truring into white and black

She felt hollow, like an empty shell

and inside her, everything was dark

Her happiness and smile

got sealed in her lips

Her soul trying to find solace in solitude

by burning all the witness of her heartbreaking memories.

Little Things

Somedays, to feel better,

I want a little coffee.

And lots of cuddles from you

I love how we enjoy eachother's company

I rethink those moments we spent together,

even if those are few

It's amazing how I feel calm

Only by looking into your eyes

Do you know, even just by your touch,

my stomach gets full of butterflies

I feel like my heart was starving for your love since ages

You light up my day with your liitle compliments

You made my heart and soul free which was trapped in cages

Scars

Yes, I want to see you happy

I know you are messed up and broken

Tell me about all the feelings buried inside you

The words which are left unspoken

I know I can't take anyone's place

I just want to see your smiling face

Everyday I see you hurting yourself

Sometimes crying loud

Trying to get over, move on

But again falling on the ground

It will take sometime

Because I know how you feel

But all it takes is to be strong, keep patience

The scars will definitely heal

Let me be the one

Let me be the one,

whom you call when you are upset

Let me be the one to console you

make you understand,

"failure isn't final, you just need to reset"

Let me be your best friend , your lover

Let me be your diary, secret keeper

Let me be the one who brongs a smile on your lips

I know I am not your first,

But let me be your last kiss

I promise, I will be with you

even when you are in a mess

Let me be the one to guide you in the darkness

Let me hold you close whenever you feel lonely

Stay with me forever,

Let me be your one and only

Essence of your love

Absorbing the essence of your love

walking near the ocean

under the clear night sky

stars shining above

looking into eachother's eyes

I want my tomorrow to wait

I want to relive this moment again

whenever I am with you

The feelings I feel

Is always more than great

Paper

Constantly ignored, misjudged again

wrote all the feelings in the paper

crumbled it and threw

all my hopes broken

tears on the cheeks

some drops on the ink

suddenly everything changed in a blink

feels like I am stuck in an empty room

am trying to escape

but couldn't get away

drenched in my memories

the words turned magically into rhymes

and verses flow in most mystic way

Sunbeam

You tiptoed in the midnight into my dreams

breaking through the darkness

just like the rays of morning sunbeams

my heart bloomed just like sunflower

faced toward that light

my heart craves always for your presence

hold me close and never go away from my sight

If I want my future to be with you

Will you help me?

With thousands of tomorrows

We will forget all our sorrows

In every morning, your face is the first thing I want to see

My lips shall breathe in your kiss

With you beside, I could find light even in eclipse

Open Book

Since the first day

all my poems are about you

You found so may sides of me

which I never knew

Made me believe in miracles

Held my hand and helped me walk through

When all I was getting from

life was bricks and pebbles

You even understood my silence

You loved me the way I am,

never asked me to change

Everytime you look into my eyes

It feels like you are looking into my heart

Reading all my secrets and all my stories

You are the one for whom,

I am an open book, never a mystrey

Breeze

I am gazing at the clear sky thinking about you

The moon is so beautiful and bright today,

like a beautiful painting on a canvas of blue

It feels like the moon and those infinite stars smiling back at me

Your love is just like this breeze which is flowing by touching

every inch of my soul even though I can't see

It makes me alive again.

I know we are miles apart.

Still I can feel your love to the core of my heart

Sapling

When you came into my life

you have cultivated a flower sapling

everyday you make me smile

And my happiness acts like sun

Now, it grows inside me

everyday just like your love

It was worth waiting for you

Because you made me feel this

beautiful feeling

Longing for you

Sometimes I am unable to

explain my longing for you

Sometimes some emotions I feel

I have never felt, they are new

I can't describe these words

it's like a different language

only my heart know

I wish if there is any other possible

ways I could show

In middle of so much chaos

my eyes only sees you,

my strength, where I belong

No matter what people say

You will be always present in my

every thoughts, every breath,

every poems and every song

Those Eyes

You got this look in your eyes

when I look at them

So deep, just like ocean

I swim sometimes

and sometimes I get lost

Everytime I get mesmerise

I am transparent to you

You know my soul more than I do.

Morning like this

Peeping through the window

between the curtains

morning sun shining all the way

me laying on your chest

a morning forehead kiss is the best way

to start my day

cuddling little bit more in your arms

wishing to stop the flow of time

Looking at your face

admiring every bit of it,

thinking to myself "thank god! he is mine"

This is the way I fall in love

with you all over again

More and more everyday.

You are my king baby.

My heart is your kingdom where you reign.

You are enough

Even after you leave the bed

I can feel te traces of your touch on my skin

Everytime I see into your eyes,

why I haven't we met earlier

All these years, where have you been

Do you remember the moments

when you held my waist,

let me stand on your feet

Those moments were so perfect and precious

that whenever I am sad,

I recall those in my mind on repeat

Sometimes, when you hug me

I feel like my life sums up right there, in your arms

You are enough, your love is enough for my existence

Since the day I loved you,

you are present in all my wishes and prayers.

Let me

Sometimes my words are not enough

to make you feel my love

They say, love is meant to be felt.

So, let me kiss your lips,

let me show you how much my skin

craves to get explored by your finger tips

When everything is said and done,

let me cuddle in your arms.

I feel safe and calm

I find peace and comfort

I feel like I am in a different place

where nobody and nothing

can cause me any harm

Bound

The tiptoe kisses, the laughter we share

The little things we do together

shows how much we care

When you are beside,

my heart feels safe and sound

I know you are the one

to whom I am bound

Everyday I wish lifelong happiness for us

You are my beginning, my end,

my everything

My life revolves around you

You are my whole universe

Sunset

I love sunset

Everybody returns back to their families

even birds return back to their nest

At this time of the day

everything takes a pause for

a moment, to take some rest

But, I kove those sunsets more

when my heart, my mind

and I are at the same place

When my love is right in front of

me with open arms

and I can just run and hug him tight

makes me forget all the

anxiety, pain and stress

Gestures

Whenever we meet

the smile I see on your lips

the happiness I see

in those dazzling eyes

nothing else matters for that moment

It is enough to make my day

I love when you pinch my cheeks

kiss me and suddenly start teasing me

Even if we talk for hours

There always a lot of things

I wanted to say

I wish we could take a break

from every responsibilities,

and go for a long drive

Everyday feels like burden now.

With you and only you I feel alive

Knot

The string from my heart

is entangled with yours

The knot of love and understanding

we have is never going to break by any force

I'll keep holding your hands through every seasons

Suddenly, my perspective towards life has changed

My mind is always occupied by your thoughts

there is a blush on my cheeks and

a smile on my lips more often

Everything seems beautiful.

And you are the only reason

Rock Bottom

They say when you hit rock bottom

it hits you hard

it hits you the most

The worst gets over

It changes you

Just like the phoenix rises from ash

You get better than what have you lost

Never forget, there is always a chance to start over

That's when hope starts working

Even if you fall, you have to get up

Get yourself together and always keep moving

Imagination

Just like demons and evils lurking in the shadows

Her worries and traumas are always there

She still manages to hide them

behind that beautiful but forced smile

Never she shows what bothers her

Never she shows how much she care

Wrapped herself with thorns

in isolation, she mourns

Her saviour was her imagination

She use it against the reality as her weapon

Silence

Knocking everyone out

She locked herself in that vaccant room

Embraced all the darkness and silence

Although, she wanted to open up,

scream and shout

She caressed all her bruises

covered all the wounds

Neither she wanted to bother nor

wanted any acknowledgement

She pulled a mask on her

sorrow with fake smile,

kindness and love with

jealousy and selfishness

Till today, her beautiful soul

was never found

Her Presence

He has survived all the seasons

summer, rain, winter and autumn

with his thoughts, hopes and dreams

hidden inside him always

Got lost thousand times,

But again found his ways

Never he thought,

he would cross paths with her

She will enter his life so unexpectedly

His world got upside down suddenly

He found his home in her

where he could confide himself

He had no fear until he only feared

to loose the warmth of her presence

Even in a crowd of thousands,

he felt lonely only in her absence

I Wish

I am jealous from the morning sun

who can see you everyday

even when am not around

I am jealous of everyone who hear

your voice before I could listen your sound

I wish I could be the sunlight so that I

could embrace you whenever you go

I wish I could be a star on the night sky,

I would twinkle to cheer you up

whenever you miss me and feel low

Long Distance

They asked her, " what is the most valuable gift he has given to you?"

She replied with a smile on her lips

and sparkles in her eyes, "memories"

They have a lot of memories to hold on to

Whenever they look at eachother in those video calls

their eyes speaks more than the words could ever do

Stories they want to share, emotions they feel,

how much they care

in every specific unique ways

Even if they are miles away

Even if they have nothing to say

Your Name

Your name is not just a name

For me, it's an emotion

It's printed on my mind, my heart,

on every inch of my skin

My heart is with you

I love every parts, every phases

every shades of yours

When I met you, I didn't knew

the best part of my life has just begun

Somedays your name makes me smile,

I get stuck in our memories for a while,

thinking about your eyes,

your hands holding mine,

And our late night conversation

Forever

He liked the way how her hairs

    falls on her shoulder,

    It reminds him how the sunrays

    spills in the woods

    Her touch makes him feel the warmth

    of the sun in winter

    Her fragrance felt like summer breeze

    Makes him happy

    Put his heartbeats on ease

    They overcome all their obstacles together

    They define the word "forever"

9 798888 555173